The Sinning Saint

By Lamar West

Copyright 2019 by Lamar West

All rights reserved. No portion of this book may be reproduced, stored, recreated or transmitted in any form or by any means-electronic, mechanical, photocopy, recording, scanning, or other-except for brief quotations in reviews or articles, without the prior written permission from the publisher.

Published in Chester, Virginia, by HDP Writings LLC.

For any inquiries please email
HDPWritingsLLC@gmail.com

Scripture and/or notes quoted by permission. Quotations designated (NET) are from the NET Bible® copyright ©1996-2016 by Biblical Studies Press, L.L.C. All rights reserved.

To the reader,

    This book was created for you, so you can know there is no space too far or dark for God's love to reach you.

    Each poem expresses the most intimate and soul wrenching thoughts, of a person on their quest to find Jesus.

    The poems represent you speaking to God, the bible scriptures are God replying to you through his words. A conversation between you and the Creator. There is nothing off limits.

    I pray for each of you, I hope you find the answers you seek.

It is my honor and privilege to introduce you to, *The Sinning Saint.*

Lamar West

Acknowledgements

A special thanks to those who played a role in the process of me growing and creating this book. I dove to the most deep and challenging pits of my spirit, to create this piece. Thank you to <u>my parents</u> Milton and Cassina West. My older brother Milton and my older sister Mika. Thanks to Phillip Noel, Everette Taylor, Cornelius Lindsey, Creyonta West, Iona Beasley, Andrea Moncada, Jennifer Montano, Samaiyah Williams, Derrick Godette and The 400 Family. Thanks to all of my family and friends.

I went to hell and came back with the devil's head.

"I am able to do all things through the one who strengthens me."
Philippians 4:13

In this darkness,
my demons and scars seem to be the only things that understand me.

"And no wonder, for even Satan disguises himself as an angel of light."
2 Corinthians 11:14

My spirit has been crying,
My conscience has been dying.

"Anxiety in a person's heart weighs him down, but an encouraging word brings him joy."
Proverbs 12:25

Filled with grief from the past, I'd found a home in my sorrow and heartache. Suffering felt common.

"I relied completely on the 𝓛𝓞𝓡𝓓, and he turned toward me and heard my cry for help. He lifted me out of the watery pit, out of the slimy mud. He placed my feet on a rock and gave me secure footing."
Psalms 40:1-2

There feels like a void between God and I.
I reminisce on times where God was my dearest **friend**.
Now my savior seems to be miles away. I am **lost** without you.

"For you, 𝓛𝓞𝓡𝓓, do not abandon those who seek your help."
Psalms 9:10

Oh Lord, I know you have called me to do great things. Daily I question myself trying to determine if I am delaying my blessings, or if this is your timing. My life doesn't reflect the uniqueness you've placed in my heart. Why must I endure so much failure, is this punishment, or is this the process to becoming great?

"From everyone who has been given much, much will be required, and from the one who has been entrusted with much, even more will be asked."
Luke 12:48

This feeling is immense.
This feeling is intense.
I pray it's just a phase.

"Look, I am about to do something new…"
Isaiah 43:19

I went to war with myself, for you.

"She said to him, "How can you say, 'I love you', when you will not share your secret with me? Three times you have deceived me and have not told me what makes you strong."
Judges 16:15

There was no alcohol to numb my pain. There was no drug to fix my heartache. There was no sex to kill my lust. There was nothing, to fill the void inside of me. The burden was too much to bear. I had plunged into the depths of the most severe hurt and brokenness. Death seemed like a gift. The hole in my heart ruined me.

"I am dazed and completely humiliated, all day long I walk around mourning. For i am overcome with shame and my whole body is sick. I a numb with pain and severely battered; I groan loudly because of the anxiety I feel."
Psalms 38:6-8

14

I thought your love would heal me.
I thought your love could breathe life back into me.

"And to all these virtues add love, which is the perfect bond."
Colossians 3:14

Oh God, **where are you**? I spend nights with my mind **tormented**, with radical thoughts of trying to understand my purpose in life. Daily I seek guidance. **What is my purpose?** What shall I do next? **I need answers my lord.**

"Jesus answered and said to him, 'What I am doing you do not understand now, but you will know after this.'"
John 13:7

Me loving you, gave me hope that I could one day give myself that same love.

"The one who acquires wisdom loves himself.."
Proverbs 19:8

I thought this person was from you, God. This mirage seemed like a prayer answered from heaven, a gift. This painful love can't be from you, yet I still want it. I beg you for it. Now, my heart and soul is drained. Why did you send them, Lord? How do I recover..

"Dear friends, do not believe every spirit, but test the spirits to determine if they are from God."
1 John 4:1

Distress and uneasiness rattles my peace.
A coat of botherism crawls on me.
Not knowing if this is my fear,
or you telling me this is wrong.

"The human mind is more deceitful than anything else. It is incurably bad. Who can understand it?"
Jeremiah 17:9

Is this my heart speaking,
or has the world tainted me.

"Because all that is in the world (the desire of the eyes and the arrogance produced by material possession) is not from the Father, but is from the world."
1 John 2:16

In this isolation, I long for you.
I need isolation, to battle my innermost thoughts.
Sometimes seclusion does me well.

"Instead he finds pleasure in obeying the LORD's commands; he meditates on his commands day and night."
Psalms 1:2

I've looked all my demons in the face.
I knew them, they were people.

"Be sober and alert. Your enemy the devil, like a roaring lion, is on the prowl looking for someone to devour."
1 Peter 5:8

Nobody, can understand what I am feeling inside.
I don't even understand it.

"They are from the world; therefore they speak from the world's perspective…We are from God..."
1 John 4:5-6

I hate the things that I do,
yet I continue to do them.

"For I do not do the good I want,
but I do the very evil I do not want!"
Romans 7:19

A sin should be a mistake,
not an intention.
My sinful ways displease my spirit.

"Everyone who has been fathered by God does not practice sin, because God's seed resides in him, and thus he is not able to sin, because he has been fathered by God." - 1 John 3:9

I'm misunderstood, I don't fit in this world.
Who will accept me?
Will I feel this way forever?

We know that we are from God, and the whole
world lies in the power of the evil one.
1 John 5:19

My anger toward God has flooded me with guilt. My hatred toward myself has engulfed me in shame. Angry at myself, angry at the world, or angry at God. Sometimes I can't tell the difference.

"My God, my God, why have you abandoned me? I groan in prayer, but help seems far away. My God, I cry out during the day, but you do not answer, and during the night my prayers do not let up."
Psalms 22:1-2

My thoughts had led me astray
.I felt like I was on death row, in the devil's prison.
I was drowning in my tears, I was strangled by my fears.
I was tired of being broken, tired of carrying around scars.
I was tired of this dark cloud over me, tired of the devil attacking me.
I was waiting for something, or someone to save me.
Healing seemed impossible.
I asked what I did to deserve this pain.
I'd forgotten all the blessings he had bestowed upon me.
I was scared to hold myself accountable for all the mistakes I brung upon myself.
I didn't have the strength to survive one more day.
All I had left were my desperate cries to God.
This was it, I was going to take matters into my own hands..
And suddenly God rescued me.
He helped me let go of the past.
He cleansed me of all sin. Removed all my scars.
Accept that I can't control the outcome.
The answer wasn't a relationship, money or sex.
It was simply, to **surrender**.
Allow God to cleanse you of the pain, allow him to renew your mind and spirit.

Surrender.

And once I surrendered,
I realized everything I desired was in the hands of God.

"Then you will take delight in the Lord, and he will answer your prayers."
Psalms 37:4

All the magnificent and glorious things they said about Jesus were true. I became a witness.

"The godly cry out and the Lord hears; he saves them from all their troubles."
Psalms 34:17

Jesus saved me from the depths of my despair and darkness.
He patched my wounds and healed my broken heart.

"The Lord is near the brokenhearted, he delivers those who are discouraged."
Psalms 34:18

The devil almost had me

"Clothe yourselves with the full armor of God so that you may be able to stand against the schemes of the devil."
Ephesians 6:11

There is nothing between heaven and earth, that can detach me from your love. There is no sin too severe, no mistake too costly, no deed too wrong, that will remove your love.

"For I am convinced that neither death, nor life, nor angels, nor heavenly rules, nor things that are present, nor thing to come, nor powers, nor height, nor depth, not anything else in creation will be able to seperate us from the love of God in Christ Jesus our Lord."
Romans 8:38

The peace you fill me with is not fathomable to the human mind.
Having your peace, is having heaven.

"Let the peace of Christ be in control of your heart (for you were in fact called as one body to this peace), and be thankful."
Colossians 3:15

Your strength fights the battles that are beyond my limitations.
I seek your supernatural peace in everything I do.
I search every crevice of earth for your peace.

"Seek the Lord and the strength he gives! Seek his presence continually!"
1 Chronicles 16:11

I now rest, knowing your plans are better than mine.
You've perfectly written my story from beginning to end.
Granting me the privilege to explore all you have to offer.

"Indeed, my plans are not like your plans, and my deeds are not like your deeds, for just as the sky is higher than the earth, so my deeds are superior to your deeds and my plans superior to your plans."
Isaiah 55:8-9

You turned my sorrow into joy.
You turned my pain into peace.
You turned my anger into love.

"Now may the Lord of peace himself give you peace at all times and in every way. The Lord be with you all."
2 Thessalonians 3:16

I kneel at the feet of Jesus.
And for that, he stands up to my biggest problems

"Do not be afraid of them, for the Lord your God will
personally fight for you."
Deuteronomy 3:22

I speak life into the dreams and desires you fill me with.
Knowing that by my faith, and your power...they will come to pass.

"Then you will take delight in the *Lord*, and he will answers your prayers."
Psalms 37:4

My desire for Christ, is my biggest strength.
My desire to have faith in God, was already enough faith.

"I have asked the Lord for one thing, this is what I desire! I want to live in the Lord's house all the days of my life, so I can gaze at the splendor of the Lord and contemplate in his temple."
Psalms 27:4

You gave me everything I needed.
It surpassed everything I wanted.

"And my God will supply your every need according to
his glorious riches."
Phillipians 4:19

Once I surrendered and gave everything to Jesus,
I saw the power of Jesus in everything.

"But above all pursue his kingdom and righteousness and all these things will be given to you as well."
Matthew 6:33

42

I wanted my prayers answered and handed to me on a silver platter. Instead you granted me the chance to be a witness to your work, and watch the process of prayers going from imagination to life.

"O LORD WHO RULES OVER ALL, how blessed are those who trust in you!"
Psalms 84:12

In order to give birth to the new me, I had to bury the old me. All of the lingering unhealthy scars, trauma and ill desires. My new life, costed me my old life. My old habits were replaced by new habits. My old scars, were replaced by new ambitions. My old self was strong and courageous, teaching me life lessons that I still cherish. However, my heart is now in the hands of the almighty.

"Then Jesus said to his disciple, 'If anyone wants to become my follower, he must deny himself, take up his cross, and follow me.'"
Matthew 16:24

Everything I prayed for was given to me, but through a process.
I received everything I asked the Lord for, yet they were revealed to me in ways that my eyes did not first recognize.

"For everything there is an appointed time, and an appropriate time for every activity on earth."
Ecclesiastes 3:1

The things you've done in my life are so magnificent, that your hand on my life is evident. You've blessed me so significantly that every creation knows, this blessing was from the creator of the universe. I can not take credit for the good in my life, you deserve all the praise. The blessings you give me, leave everyone as a witness to your power and glory.

"for the one bringing forth in you both the desire and the effort, for the sake of his good pleasure is God."
Philippians 2:13

Faith is the single most important thing in life.

"Now faith is being sure of what we hope for, being convicted of what we do not see."
Hebrew 11:1

I have learned,
that your forgiveness and love conquers anything
of this world.
There is no better cure than love.

"Instead, be kind to one another, compassionate,
forgiving one another, just as God in Christ also forgave
you."
Ephesians 4:32

Although I've failed 1,000 times, I take joy in knowing I've tried 1,000 times. Better it is, to try and fail. Then never try at all. Better it is, to love and fail, then to never love at all. My courage is commendable.

"Although a righteous person may fall seven times, he gets up again, but the wicked will be brought down by calamity."
Proverbs 24:16

I still struggle. At times it feels like my thoughts are from the devil.
My mind is in bondage, enslaved to doubt.
Questioning my purpose, my life, my existence.
The darkness is trying to come back.

"The one who is spiritual discerns all things, yet he himself is understood by no one.
For who has known the mind of the Lord, so as to advise him?
But we have the mind of Christ."
1 Corinthians 2:15-16

```
Hoping that I can capture and store
this moment of peace for the rest of
               my days.
Your peace surpasses everything else.
```

"Let the peace of Christ be in control in your heart (for you were in face called as one body to his peace), and be thankful."
Colossians 3:15

The freedom I seek, comes from **Christ**. When I allow my spirit to lead me, I find freedom and peace in everything. I feel **NO** walls. I enjoy the beauties of life as I feel kinder, wiser, and more gentle. Letting my spirit lead me allows me to become the person you **CREATED** me to be.

"But the fruit of the Spirit is love, joy, peace, patience, kindness, goodness, faithfulness, gentleness, and self-control. Against such things there is no law."
Galatians 5:22

The life inside of me, has been peeled away. My mind, heart and spirit lay in decay.
I spend each day, searching for something to resurrect the inner me.
I cannot find the words to pray.
Hoping you can hear the prayers that I cannot utter.
Don't let the darkness come back God..

"In the same way, the Spirit helps us in our weakness, for we do not know how we should pray, but the Spirit himself intercedes for us with inexpressible groanings."
Romans 8:26

Today is **your** day. God has dedicated all of his focus on **you**.
Today is the day you receive every blessing that's **yours**.

"constantly pray"
1 Thessalonians 5:17

I met you in the tenderness and innocence of my youth.
Yearning for love, I found it in you.
You were one of my earliest gifts from God. You nurtured my spirit, I cherish you forever.

"Surging waters cannot quench love; flood waters cannot overflow it. If someone were to offer all his possessions to buy love, the offer would be utterly despised."
Song of Solomon 8:7

Depressive thoughts roaring, with the devils pain raging against my peace.
The storm is so dark I cannot see, but still I feel your presence.
Your peace is reachable in any circumstance.
Don't let it come back.

"Even though I must walk through the darkest valley, I fear no danger, for you are with me; your rod and your staff reassure me."
Psalms 23:4

Don't let the darkness come back, God.

Your radiant light shined,
right after my darkest night.

"I sought the Lord's help and he answered me; he delivered me from all my fears."
Psalms 34:4

I thought I was healed. Now my heart thirst for love.
I am desperate for affection.

"'Yes, I will restore you to health. I will heal your wounds. I, the LORD, affirm it!'"
Jeremiah 30:17

"'When an unclean spirit goes out of a person, it passes through waterless places looking for rest but does not find it. Then it says, 'I will return to the home I left'. When it returns, it finds the house empty, swept, clean and put in order. Then it goes and brings seven other spirits more evil than itself, and they go in and live there, so the last state of the person is worse than the first.'"

Matthew 12:43-45

```
The joy you gave me, crunched any
       sorrow I had ever felt.
This joy is everlasting. This joy is
          here to stay.
```

"In a far-off land the LORD will manifest himself on them. He will say to them, 'I have loved you with an everlasting love. That is why I have continued to be faithful to you.'"
Jeremiah 31:3

And now it's hard not to spend the day smiling, when I feel God's love and grace.
As if it was embedded in the wind.
It's hard to not smile when I think of all God has done for me.

"Give thanks to the LORD,
for he is good and his loyal love endures."
1 Chronicles 16:34

I smile to the melody of your voice.
You listen to the hymn of my prayers.

"The prayer of a righteous person has great effectiveness."
James 5:16

On this mysterious and wondrous journey,
I tour this place you have created,
on a voyage to find you in everything I do.

"I love those who love me,
and those who seek me find me."
Proverbs 8:17

Hanging on to every inch of hope and faith left inside me, knowing that your plans and intentions are better than I could ever imagine. My faith, is all that I have left.

"'For I know what I have planned for you,' says the Lord. 'I have plans to prosper you, not to harm you. I have plans to give you a future filled with hope.'"
Jeremiah 29:11

My dreams were mere fantasies,
unreachable ideas that seemed like
nothing more than vivid imaginations.
Until I placed them in your hands.

"But above all pursue his kingdom and
righteousness and all these things will be given to
you as well."
Matthew 6:33

My heart is filled with ambitions, wisdom and optimism.
My expectations to attain my aspirations are high, because I believe in you.

"Ask and it will be given to you; seek and you will find; knock and the door will be opened for you. For everyone who asks receives..."
Matthew 7:7-8

When I step outside my comfort zone, when I step beyond my limitations and boundaries, that's when I step into your hands. When I solely rely on my trust in you, thats where your power marvels the most. When I believe in your capabilities even when I can't see them, that's when you do things beyond my power. Your miracles lies in unfamiliarity.

"for we live by faith, not by sight."
2 Corinthians 5:7

All of my demons have become a distant memory, that I don't want to remember. I can see my promising future through my windshield of faith. While my rearview has become too small, to reflect on my past.

"'Don't remember these earlier events; don't recall these former events. Look, I am about to do something new."
Isaiah 43:18-19

There is no certainty in the plans of my future,
but there is certainty God will be with me.

"Your word is a lamp to walk by, and a light to
illuminate my path."
Psalms 119:105

Am I really healed?

You delivered me from the valley. You pulled me up this slippery slope. Now I rest at the top of your mountain

"They cried out to the LORD in their distress; he delivered them from their troubles."
Psalms 107:6

The person I am now feels like a stranger, a glimpse of who I used to be.

"Do not be conformed to this present world,
but be transformed by the renewing of your mind,
so that you may test and approve what is the will of
God…"
Romans 12:2

I'm tired of being used and disposed of. This anger inside of me is coming back, God.

My uniqueness is not accidental.
All of my flaws are a canvas for you to display your love and power.

"But he said to me, 'My grace is enough for you, for my power is made perfect in weakness.' So then, I will boast most gladly about my weaknesses, so that the power of Christ may reside in me."
Corinthians 12:9

When I look back on my life, I cannot take credit for anything.
You receive all the glory. For my strength alone fails me.
My wisdom alone, leads to poor decisions.
Yet you cover me every time.

"He is the one you should praise; he is your God, the one who has done these great and awesome things for you that you have seen."
Deuteronomy 10:21

Although I've neglected you,
although I've ventured off to explore my own desires.
I always find myself coming back home to you.
Thankful that you have never sent me away.

"I will never leave you nor forsake you"
Joshua 1:5

If I had all the answers, there'd be no need for faith. There is no one exclusive formula to this journey. Your powers exceed my limits of thinking. I find myself lost and distraught, trying to figure out my way in life. But that's when my faith and trust in you becomes beautiful. My weaknesses and ignorance, strengthen my faith and dependency on you. I don't just believe in you, I depend on you. Knowing that this journey of life is difficult, knowing that I don't have the answers. But, I know the person who does.

"Trust in the Lord with all your heart, and do not rely on your own understanding. Acknowledge him in all your ways, and he will make your paths straight."
Proverbs 3:5

I'm still fighting, Lord. I can not give up!
You've brung me this far, I can not quit.

I can now say that I've experienced the presence of God. God is truly better than anything of this earth. The mere feeling, the mere smell of our creator is beyond greater than any miracle imaginable to the mind. There has never been, and never will be anything worthy of comparison to the presence of God. Seek him, with all of your heart.

"O Lord, you are great, mighty, majestic, glorious and sovereign over all the sky and earth! You have dominion and exalt as the ruler of all."
1 Chronicles 29:11

This world isn't enough for me. This world doesn't fulfill my soul completely. People, places and things bring me a joy, but not the ultimate everlasting joy that I seek. Cliche quotes don't satisfy the inner most intimate pieces of my spirit. I need wisdom that only you provide. I am in search for something greater, I am in search of God. The one who created me.

"Do not love the world or the things in the world. If anyone loves the world, the love of the Father is not in him, because all that is in the world (the desire of the flesh and the desire of the eyes and the arrogance produced by material possessions) is not from the Father, but is from the world."
1 John 2:15-16

I love you so much. That I want you, to love God more than you love me. I want you to love yourself more than you love me. Your spirit belongs to Christ. He's simply granted me the gift of intertwining our lives and our souls.

I am obsessed with God. I am obsessed with my pursuit of peace and purpose. Yet I've become attached to the things that pull me away from him. Yet I've become addicted and infatuated with the shallow ways of this world. Chasing God, while chasing things of this world, leave me conflicted.

"For what does it benefit a person if he gains the whole world but forfeits his life?..."
Matthew 16:26

"But above all pursue his kingdom and righteousness and all these things will be given to you as well."
Matthew 6:33

You have somehow used everything in my life,
to mold me into the beautiful person that I am today.
Although I perceived my darkest times as punishment, you've used those times to enhance me. Even the problems I've brung upon myself, through your grace you have used those mistakes to help make me the person I want to be. Using every piece of my story for good.

"And we know that all things work together for good for those who love God, who are called according to his purpose..."
Romans 8:28

I'm grateful, that your love, grace and patience is everlasting.
Thankful that your love has no restrictions, thankful that you do not keep track of all the mistakes I've made.
Knowing that each day, your grace is renewed within me.

You know the history of my heart.
You know the small intricates lingering inside me, that
keep me fearful of being hurt again.

Pray about it.

"When you call out to me and come to me in prayer, I will hear your prayers"
Jeremiah 29:12

Walking this earth, feeling like I am destined for greatness. My belief that you've called me to do miraculous things, sits with me like the clothing on my body. I feel like I am of heavenly descent. I am humble knowing you're the master, but I am ready to walk into my greatness. Is this a false ego, or am I anointed, dear Lord?

"'Before I formed you in your mother's womb I chose you. Before you were born I set you apart. I appointed you to be a prophet of the nations.'"
Jeremiah 1:5

Lord, how is one to resist all the temptations of this world? Money excites me. Sex is attractive. The world I live in, values the opposite of your morals.

"How can a young person maintain a pure life? By guarding it according the your instructions!"
Psalms 119:9

**Stop.
Talk to God.**

My most abundant peace comes as a
result of my obedience to you.
When I follow and obey my spirit,
I feel limitless.

"For all who are led by the Spirit of God are the sons of God."
Romans 8:14

I cannot serve God and the world. I've chosen God, I've chosen to cater to my spirit above everything else. Internally I am free and in tune with my creator. Externally my discipline is weak, as I indulge in things that rebel my spirit. To have my spirit and my actions aligned with God's plan for my life, is the ultimate goal. Sometimes it feels impossible.

"But I say, live by the spirit and you will not carry out the desires of the flesh."
Galatians 5:16

God dwells inside of me through my spirit. I can feel the spirit inside me, leading me into a direction that isn't often appealing but, necessary. My body craves to please itself and the desires it has created. The desires of my spirit and the desires of my body seem to be at war, with my mind enduring all of the wounds of this battle.

"For the flesh has desires that are opposed to the Spirit, and the Spirit has desires that are opposed to the flesh, for these are in opposition to each other, so that you cannot do what you want."
Galatians 5:17

A piece of God, has a permanent home inside of me. Which is my spirit. The spirit of God is in everyone. You are with me right now in this very moment, in form of the Holy Spirit. The supernatural maker of the entire universe, dwells inside of me. Daily I lean on your guidance and teachings to carry me.

"'But the Advocate, the Holy Spirit, whom the father will send in my name, will teach you everything, and will cause you to remember everything I have said to you.'"
John 14:26

My intuition speaks things to me, that I want to be false. I can't escape the truth that my spirit plunges onto my heart. I know it is God speaking to me, but I am not yet ready for these sacrifices. Spare me, Lord. Allow things to go my way.

"But when he, the Spirit of truth, comes, he will guide you into all truth.
For he will not speak on his own authority, but will speak whenever he hears, and will tell you what is to come."
John 16:13

The life inside of me, has been peeled away.
My mind, heart and spirit lay in decay.
I spend each day, searching for something to resurrect the inner me.
I cannot find the words to pray.
Hoping you can hear the prayers that I cannot utter.

"In the same way, the Spirit helps us in our weakness, for we do not know how we should pray, but the Spirit himself intercedes for us with inexpressible groanings."
Romans 8:26

My thoughts scare me, they make me question my sanity.

"For God did not give us a Spirit of fear but of power and love and self-control."
2 Timothy 1:7

I wholeheartedly know Christ, and he knows me. I am
blessed beyond measure.
I know where peace and love resides yet I don't attain it,
this makes me even more distraught.
I am blessed, yet I still find a route to unhappiness.

"Be devoted to prayer, keeping alert in it with
thanksgiving."
Colossians 4:2

"Let the peace of Christ be in control in your heart
(for you were in fact called as one body to his peace),
and be thankful."
Colossians 3:15

My soul has found home in the most brownest places
of hibernation

"Consequently the LORD provides safety for the oppressed;
he provides safety in the times of trouble."
Psalms 9:9

Psalms 91.

The Lord's grace is his unconditional and unwary love.
His compassion and patience with his children.
His heart of forgiveness and love triumphs everything imaginable.
Ask for his grace.

"But you, O Lord, are a compassionate and merciful God. You are patient and demonstrate great loyal love and faithfulness."
Psalms 86:15

**God's love is perfect.
It is simply impossible to make God not love you.**

"Give thanks to the God of heaven,
for his loyal love endures!"
Psalms 136:26

The things I desire exceed what my hands can touch. I desire God's love, peace, patience, wisdom, discernment, joy, fulfillment, discipline and self-control.

"But the fruit of the Spirit is love, joy, peace, patience, kindness, goodness, faithfulness, gentleness and self-control."
Galatians 5:22

I dream of making you proud Jesus.
I long for the wisdom to master my journey of life.

"But if anyone is deficient in wisdom, he should ask God, who gives to all generously and without reprimand, and it will be given to him."
James 1:5

The devil hounds me daily.
Relentless attacks until I give into sin.

"So submit to God. But resist the devil and he will
flee from you."
James 4:7

I am ready, Lord.
I have been through the storm.
I am ready to receive my blessings now.

"'Ask and it will be given to you; seek and you will find'".
Matthew 7:7

You have made my process beautiful, Lord. You perfectly used my losses to craft a better soul inside of me. Every experience drew me closer to you, it planted my roots deeper into you. Now when trouble comes my way, I will stand firm because I have already been made firm in you. My roots have been planted, my tree of life can now blossom.

"Not only this, but we also rejoice in sufferings,
knowing that suffering produces endurance,
and endurance, character, and character, hope."
Romans 5:3-4

I carried around loads of insecurities and scars.
Through grace, you helped me embrace my past and my fears.
My insecurities were not an attack from you, they were tools to increase my desire and dependency on you.

"Give me your heart, my son, and let your eyes observe my ways;"
Proverbs 23:26

I used to sit on a pedestal, thinking I'd never indulge in certain things. Thinking I'd never be in certain spaces. However you allowed me to face those very issues, to humble me. Now when others face those trials, no judgement crosses my heart. I am able to boldly say, "I have been there. Through Christ, I defeated that. God loved me through it all, and he loves you too."

"God opposes the proud but gives grace to the humble."
1 Peter 5:5

"Do not judge, and you will not be judged; do not condemn,
and you will not be condemned;
forgive, and you will be forgiven.
Give, and it will be given to you."
Luke 6:37-38

I have practiced every form of sin. I never thought I'd turn to alcohol for healing. I never thought I'd find comfort in sex and pornopgrpahy. I never thought I'd want to take my own life.I'd never thought I'd face depression and anxiety. I can't tell anyone this, Christians don't feel this way. God, was something wrong with me?

"For all have sinned and fall short of the Glory of God."
Romans 3:23

"No trial has overtaken you that is not faced by others. And God is faithful: He will not let you be tried beyond what you are able to bear."
1 Corinthians 10:13

Although I am hurt, I cannot express it.
Me expressing how they've hurt me, will in return hurt them.
I care about their feelings too much, to even tell them they have hurt me.

"And the truth will set you free."
John 8:32

I am not perfect, but I know who is.
I do not have all the answers, but I know who does.
His name reigns superior to everything in existence.
His name, is Jesus Christ.

"The law of the LORD is perfect and preserves one's life.
The rules set down by the LORD are reliable and impart wisdom to the inexperienced."
Psalms 19:7

You died for me, because you knew I'd fall short.

"Because Christ also suffered once for sins,
the just for the unjust, to bring you to God."
1 Peter 3:18

I no longer carry shame and guilt. I have brung everything to you.
There is no need to hide anything from you. You already know.
You knew the issues I'd face. There is nothing that will scare you away from me.
There is nothing off limits.

"Those who look to him for help are happy;
their faces are not ashamed."
Psalms 34:5

"There is therefore now no condemnation
for those who are in Christ Jesus."
Romans 8:1

Thank you Jesus Christ. For loving me, through every flaw, every sin, every mistake. At times I love myself, at times I don't. Sometimes I am weak, sometimes I am strong. I still do not have it all figured out Lord. But I need you, I want you. I am nothing without you. Your love brings tears to my eyes. I hope I am making you proud God. I love you. Thank you, for loving this Sinning Saint.

- Lamar West.

Made in the USA
Middletown, DE
05 June 2019